AF539149

HAPPINESS IS NOT ROCKET SCIENCE

Published 2026

FiNGERPRINT!
Prakash Books

Fingerprint Publishing
@FingerprintP
@fingerprintpublishingbooks
www.fingerprintpublishing.com

ISBN: 978 93 5856 220 0

To
From

Happiness is the core ingredient in the recipe of life!

It is something we seek, but somehow always fail to catch. We explore the how, when, and where of happiness but does it need to be so complicated?

All we need to be happy is to make the most of the good times while also being able to face the unavoidable bad times.

One bad moment does not amount to a bad day; you will always have it in you to get through it. No matter what life throws at you, always remember that you are that pot of gold at the end of the rainbow.

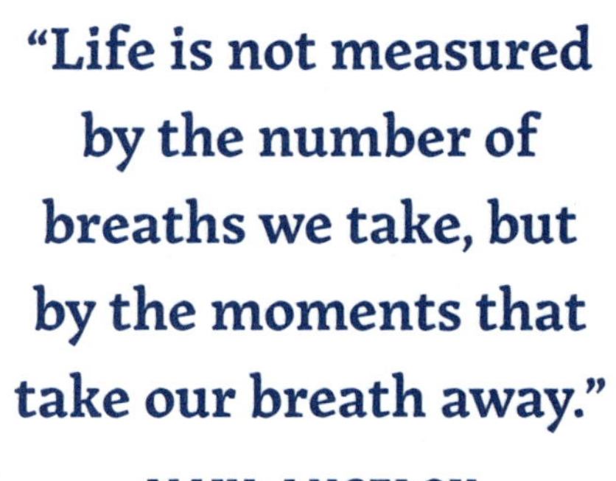

"Life is not measured by the number of breaths we take, but by the moments that take our breath away."

MAYA ANGELOU

"Not in doing what you like
but in liking what you do
is the secret of happiness."

J.M. BARRIE

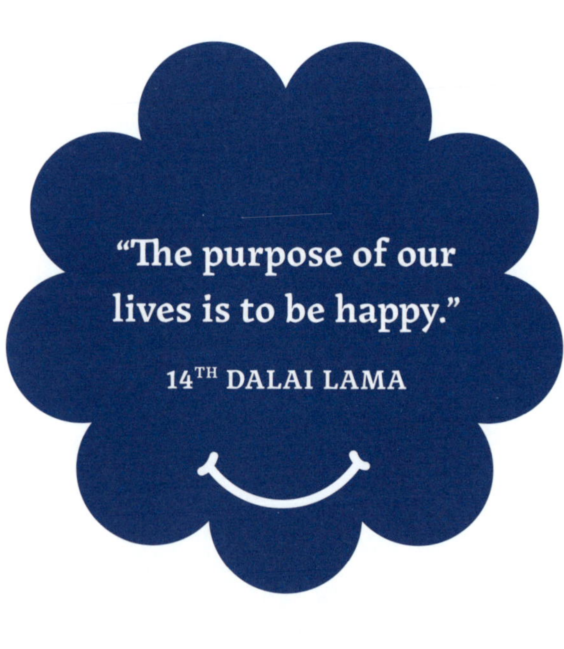
"The purpose of our lives is to be happy."
14TH DALAI LAMA

"HAPPINESS IS NOT HAVING WHAT YOU WANT, BUT WANTING WHAT YOU HAVE."

RABBI HYMAN SCHACHTEL

"THE OLDER YOU GET THE MORE YOU REALIZE THAT KINDNESS IS SYNONYMOUS WITH HAPPINESS."

LIONEL BARRYMORE

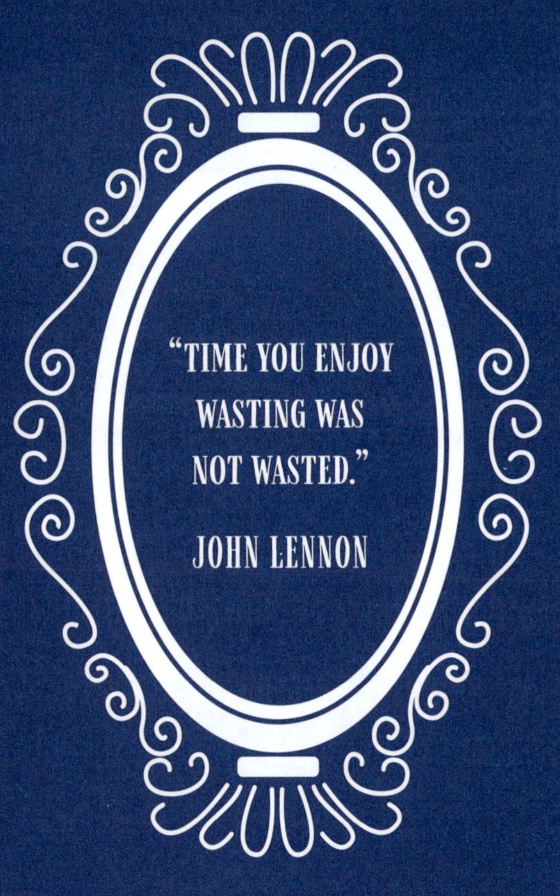
"TIME YOU ENJOY
WASTING WAS
NOT WASTED."
JOHN LENNON

“Spend your life with the person who makes you happy, not the one you have to impress.”

ANONYMOUS

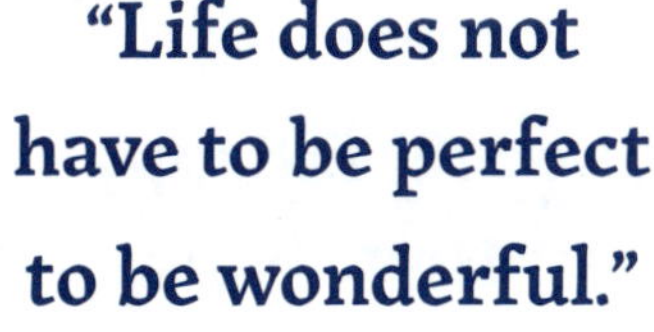

"Life does not have to be perfect to be wonderful."

ANNETTE FUNICELLO

"Whoever is happy will make others happy too."

ANNE FRANK

"Happiness makes up in height for what it lacks in length."

ROBERT FROST

“SPREAD LOVE EVERYWHERE YOU GO. LET NO ONE EVER COME TO YOU WITHOUT LEAVING HAPPIER.”

MOTHER TERESA

“HAPPINESS OFTEN SNEAKS IN THROUGH A DOOR YOU DIDN’T KNOW YOU LEFT OPEN.”

JOHN BARRYMORE

"Happiness exists on earth, and it is won through prudent exercise of reason, knowledge of the harmony of the universe, and constant practice of generosity."

JOSE MARTIN

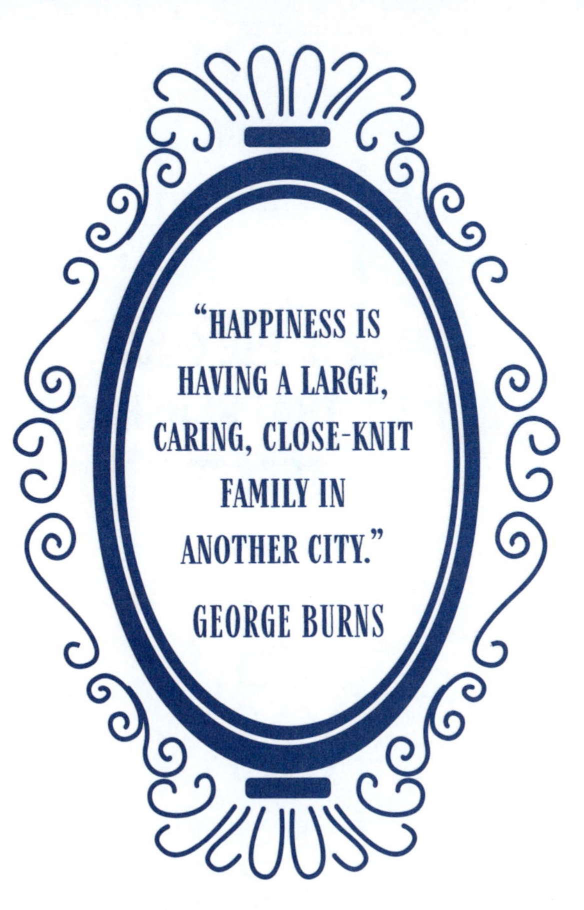
"HAPPINESS IS
HAVING A LARGE,
CARING, CLOSE-KNIT
FAMILY IN
ANOTHER CITY."
GEORGE BURNS

"MAN IS THE ONLY ANIMAL THAT BLUSHES OR NEEDS TO."

MARK TWAIN

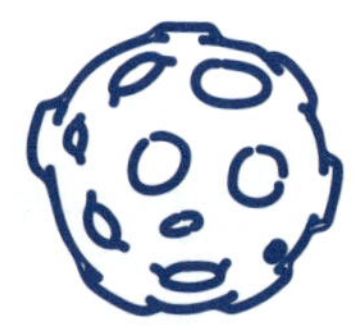

"So we shall let the reader answer this question for himself: who is the happier man, he who has braved the storm of life and lived or he who has stayed securely on shore and merely existed?"

HUNTER S. THOMPSON

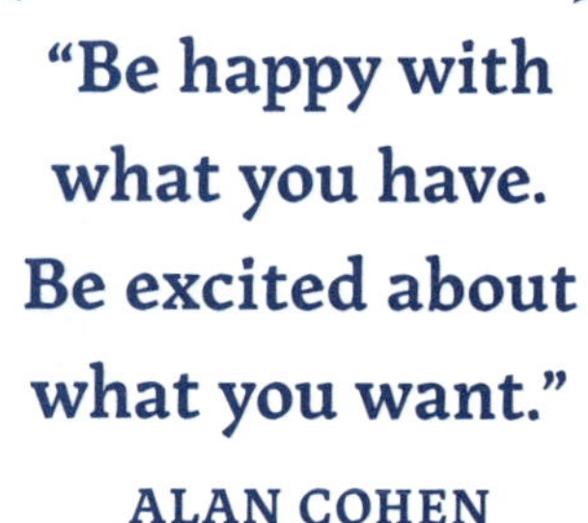
"Be happy with
what you have.
Be excited about
what you want."
ALAN COHEN

"DOING WHAT YOU LIKE IS FREEDOM. LIKING WHAT YOU DO IS HAPPINESS."

FRANK TYGER

"Sometimes the most proactive thing we can do is to be happy, just to genuinely smile."

ANONYMOUS

"If you want happiness
for an hour, take a nap.
If you want happiness
for a day, go fishing.
If you want happiness for
a year, inherit a fortune.
If you want happiness for
a lifetime, help somebody."

CHINESE PROVERB

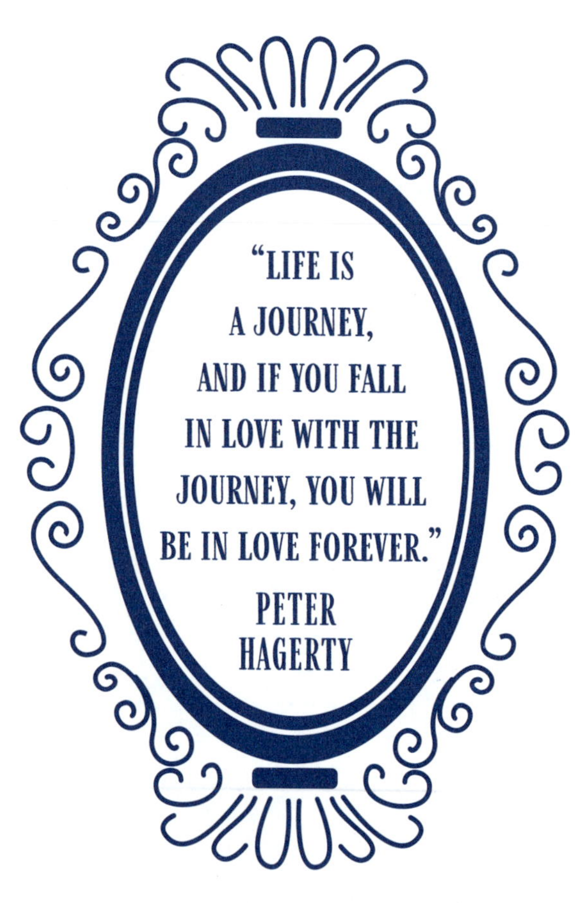
"LIFE IS
A JOURNEY,
AND IF YOU FALL
IN LOVE WITH THE
JOURNEY, YOU WILL
BE IN LOVE FOREVER."
PETER
HAGERTY

"Thousands of candles
can be lighted from
a single candle, and
the life of the candle
will not be shortened.
Happiness never decreases
by being shared."

BUDDHA

"I love those who can smile in trouble, who can gather strength from distress, and grow brave by reflection. 'Tis the business of little minds to shrink, but they whose heart is firm, and whose conscience approves their conduct, will pursue their principles unto death."

LEONARDO DA VINCI

"GREAT TRANQUILITY OF HEART IS HIS WHO CARES FOR NEITHER PRAISE NOR BLAME."

THOMAS À KEMPIS

"Each moment of
a happy lover's hour
is worth an age of dull
and common life."
APHRA BEHN

"Happiness is not a state to arrive at, but a manner of traveling."
MARGARET LEE RUNBECK

“HAPPINESS IS NOT FOUND IN THE COMPLEXITY OF EQUATIONS; IT’S THE SIMPLE ALGEBRA OF KINDNESS, MULTIPLIED BY GRATITUDE, AND DIVIDED BY THE WORRIES WE CHOOSE TO SUBTRACT FROM OUR LIVES.”

ALBERT SCHWEITZER

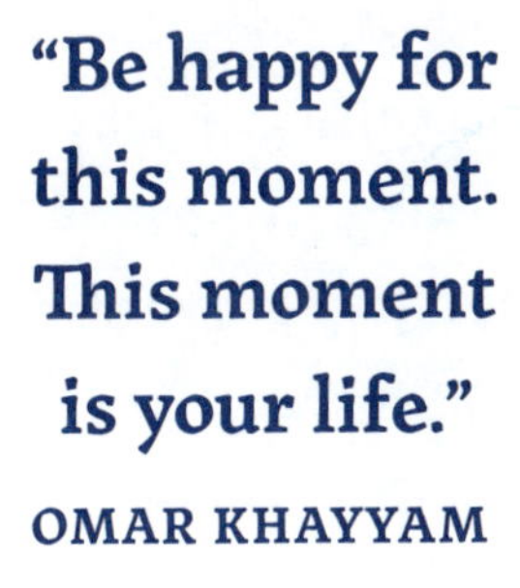

"Be happy for this moment. This moment is your life."

OMAR KHAYYAM

"DISCOVERING HAPPINESS IS NOT A ROCKET LAUNCH; IT'S THE STEADY ORBIT OF SMALL JOYS AND DAILY CHOICES, EACH ONE A TINY THRUST PROPELLING US TOWARDS A BRIGHTER UNIVERSE OF CONTENTMENT."

GRETCHEN RUBIN

"There is only one happiness in this life, to love and be loved."

GEORGE SAND

"It is not how much
we have, but how
much we enjoy, that
makes happiness."
CHARLES SPURGEON

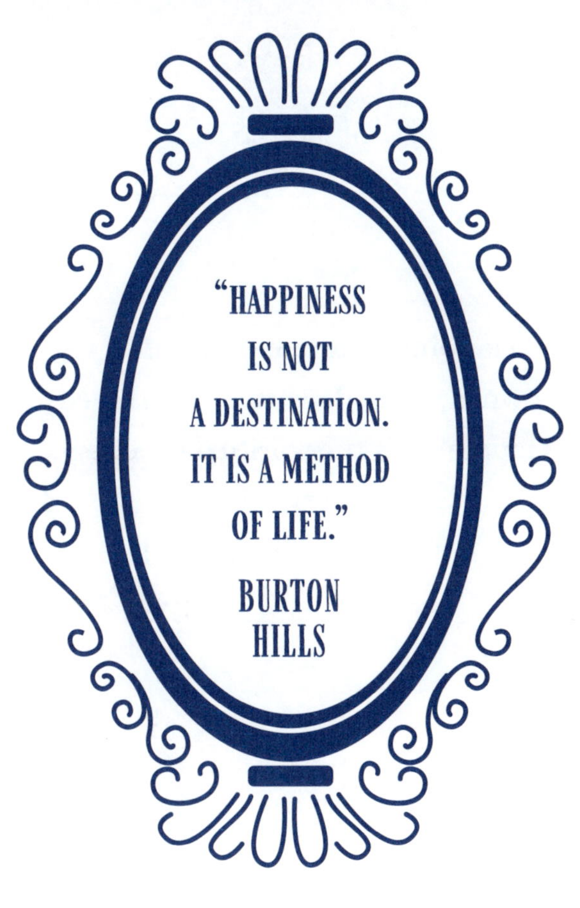
"HAPPINESS
IS NOT
A DESTINATION.
IT IS A METHOD
OF LIFE."
BURTON
HILLS

“Happiness cannot be traveled to, owned, earned, worn or consumed. Happiness is the spiritual experience of living every minute with love, grace, and gratitude.”

DENIS WAITLEY

“EVERYTHING HAS ITS WONDERS, EVEN DARKNESS AND SILENCE, AND I LEARN, WHATEVER STATE I MAY BE IN, THEREIN TO BE CONTENT.”

HELEN KELLER

“Happiness can exist only in acceptance.”

GEORGE ORWELL

"There is only one way to happiness and that is to cease worrying about things which are beyond the power of our will."

EPICTETUS

“I, not events, have the power to make me happy or unhappy today. I can choose which it shall be. Yesterday is dead, tomorrow hasn’t arrived yet. I have just one day, today, and I’m going to be happy in it.”

GROUCHO MARX

"HEALTH IS THE GREATEST GIFT, CONTENTMENT, THE GREATEST WEALTH, FAITHFULNESS, THE BEST RELATIONSHIP."

BUDDHA

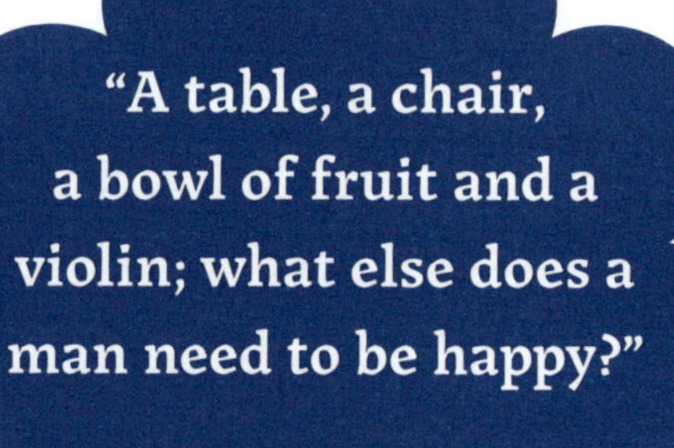
"A table, a chair,
a bowl of fruit and a
violin; what else does a
man need to be happy?"
ALBERT EINSTEIN

“When ambition ends,
happiness begins.”

THOMAS MERTON

"The science of happiness is not written in the stars; it's scripted in the choices we make, the laughter we share, and the love we cultivate in the fertile soil of our hearts."

SONJA LYUBOMIRSKY

"Now and then it's good to pause
in our pursuit of happiness
and just be happy."

GUILLAUME
APOLLINAIRE

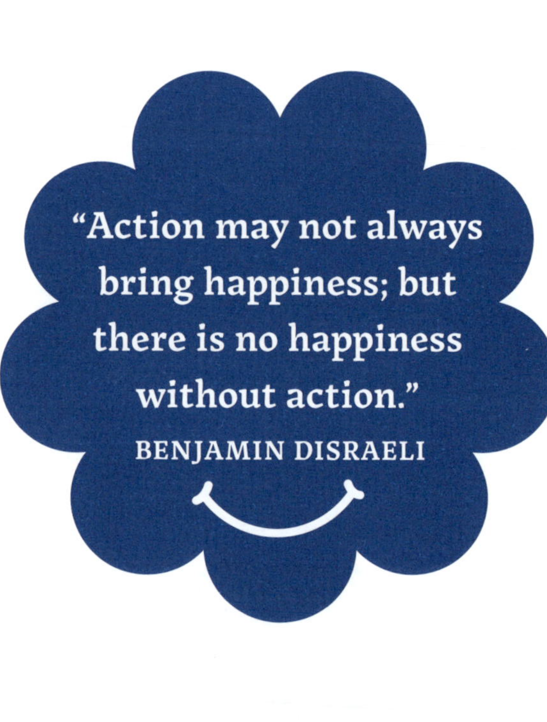
"Action may not always
bring happiness; but
there is no happiness
without action."
BENJAMIN DISRAELI

"Achievement of your happiness is the only moral purpose of your life, and that happiness, not pain or mindless self-indulgence, is the proof of your moral integrity, since it is the proof and the result of your loyalty to the achievement of your values."

AYN RAND

"Happiness is dependent on self-discipline. We are the biggest obstacles to our own happiness. It is much easier to do battle with society and with others than to fight our own nature."

DENNIS PRAGER

"To be without some of the things you want is an indispensable part of happiness."

BERTRAND RUSSELL

“HAPPINESS IS NOT A GOAL; IT IS A BY-PRODUCT.”

ELEANOR ROOSEVELT

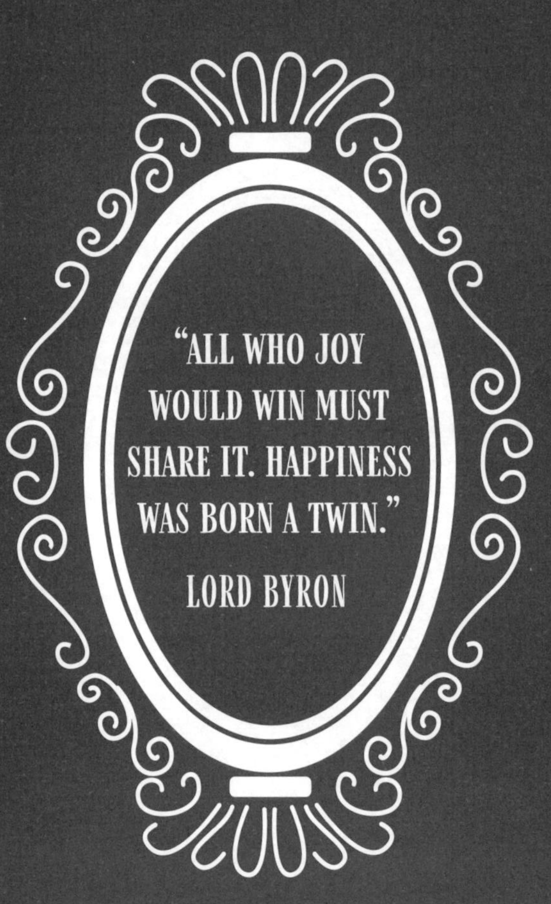
"ALL WHO JOY
WOULD WIN MUST
SHARE IT. HAPPINESS
WAS BORN A TWIN."
LORD BYRON

“HAPPINESS IS THE HARVEST OF A QUIET EYE.”

AUSTIN O’MALLEY

"The art of being happy lies in the power of extracting happiness from common things."

HENRY WARD BEECHER

"THE SECRET OF HAPPINESS IS TO ADMIRE WITHOUT DESIRING."

CARL SANDBURG

"The advantage of a bad memory is that one enjoys several times the same good things for the first time."

FRIEDRICH NIETZSCHE

"HAPPINESS ISN'T SOMETHING YOU EXPERIENCE; IT'S SOMETHING YOU REMEMBER."

OSCAR LEVANT

“Happiness is the absence of the striving for happiness.”

ZHUANGZI

"Try to make at least one person happy every day. If you cannot do a kind deed, speak a kind word. If you cannot speak a kind word, think a kind thought. Count up, if you can, the treasure of happiness that you would dispense in a week, in a year, in a lifetime!"

LAWRENCE G. LOVASIK

How to Uncomplicate Happiness?

- Go with the flow and accept life as it comes.
- Embrace the negative emotions you feel, but don't let them determine the course of your happiness.
- Don't link your happiness to the fulfillment of your desires.
- Appreciate the little things in life and share your happiness with your loved ones.
- Stop waiting around for happiness to come and live in the moment!
- Indulge in things that make you happy—read a book, watch a movie, or take a walk.
- Let things that are out of your control go!
- Focus on your health—healthy food and exercise are crucial to a happy life!

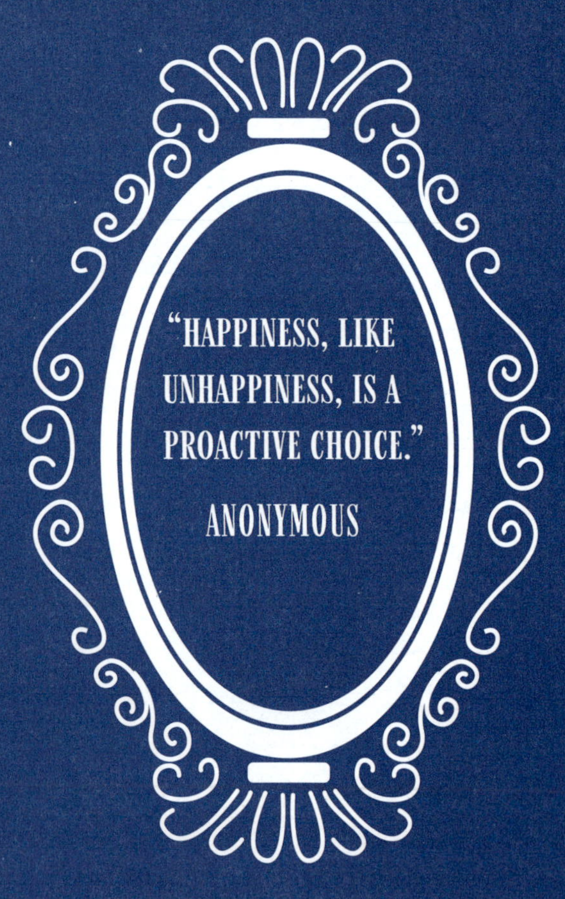
"HAPPINESS, LIKE
UNHAPPINESS, IS A
PROACTIVE CHOICE."
ANONYMOUS

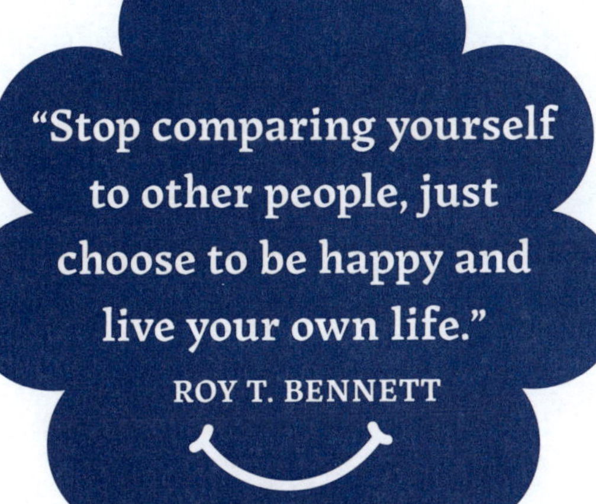
"Stop comparing yourself
to other people, just
choose to be happy and
live your own life."
ROY T. BENNETT

"HAPPINESS IS LIKE THOSE PALACES IN FAIRY TALES WHOSE GATES ARE GUARDED BY DRAGONS: WE MUST FIGHT IN ORDER TO CONQUER IT."

ALEXANDRE DUMAS

"HAPPINESS IS NOT SOMETHING YOU POSTPONE FOR THE FUTURE; IT IS SOMETHING YOU DESIGN FOR THE PRESENT."

JIM ROHN

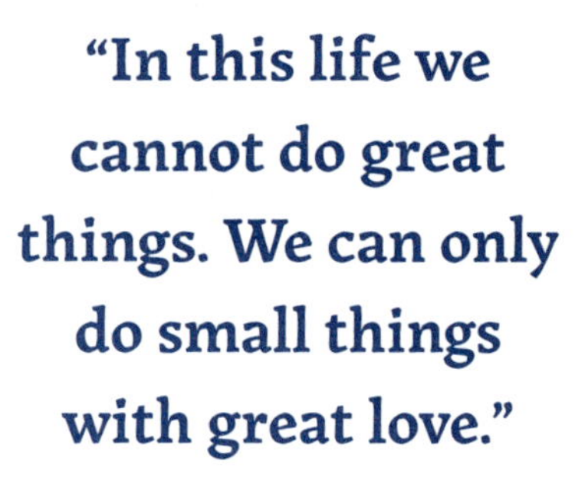

“In this life we cannot do great things. We can only do small things with great love.”

MOTHER TERESA

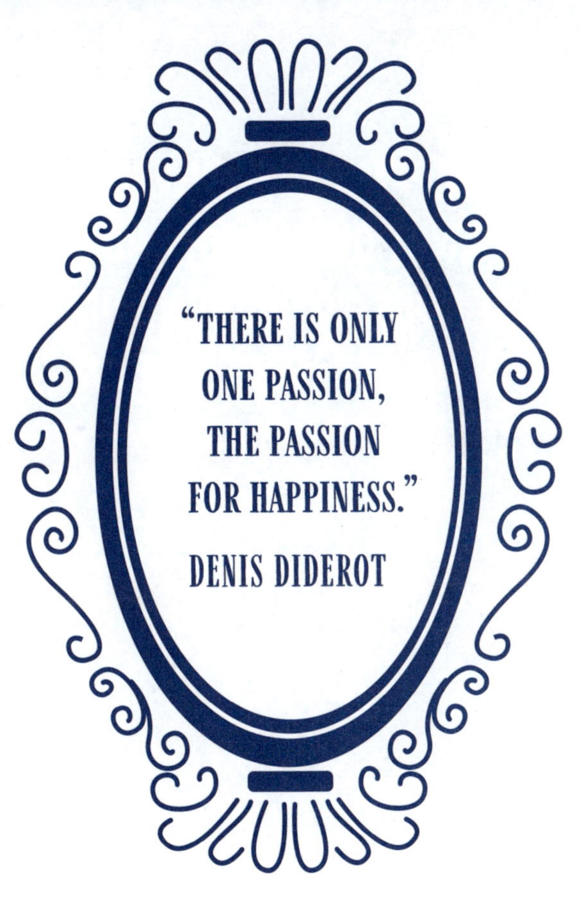
"THERE IS ONLY
ONE PASSION,
THE PASSION
FOR HAPPINESS."
DENIS DIDEROT

"HAPPINESS IS INWARD, AND NOT OUTWARD; AND SO, IT DOES NOT DEPEND ON WHAT WE HAVE, BUT ON WHAT WE ARE."

Henry Van Dyke

“ONE OF THE KEYS TO HAPPINESS IS A BAD MEMORY.”

RITA MAE BROWN

"HAPPINESS IS
GOOD HEALTH."
INGRID
BERGMAN

"Your time is limited, so don't waste it living someone else's life. Don't be trapped by dogma–which is living with the results of other people's thinking."

STEVE JOBS

“Happy is the man who has broken the chains which hurt the mind, and has given up worrying once and for all.”

OVID

"Everyone chases after happiness, not noticing that happiness is right at their heels."

BERTOLT BRECHT

"The secret of happiness is something to do."

JOHN BURROUGHS

"HAPPINESS IS A CHOICE. YOU CAN CHOOSE TO BE HAPPY. THERE'S GOING TO BE STRESS IN LIFE, BUT IT'S YOUR CHOICE WHETHER YOU LET IT AFFECT YOU OR NOT."

VALERIE BERTINELLI

"GROWTH ITSELF CONTAINS THE GERM OF HAPPINESS."

PEARL S. BUCK

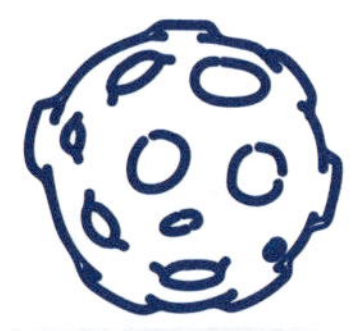

"In order to have great happiness you have to have great pain and unhappiness— otherwise how would you know when you're happy?"

LESLIE CARON

"HAPPINESS IS HARD TO RECALL. ITS JUST A GLOW."

FRANK MCCOURT

"I am a kind of paranoid in reverse. I suspect people of plotting to make me happy."

J. D. SALINGER

"A sure way to lose happiness, I found, is to want it at the expense of everything else."

BETTE DAVIS

"Joy, rather than happiness, is the goal of life, for joy is the emotion which accompanies us fulfilling our natures as human beings. It is based on the experience of one's identity as being of worth and dignity."

ROLLO MAY

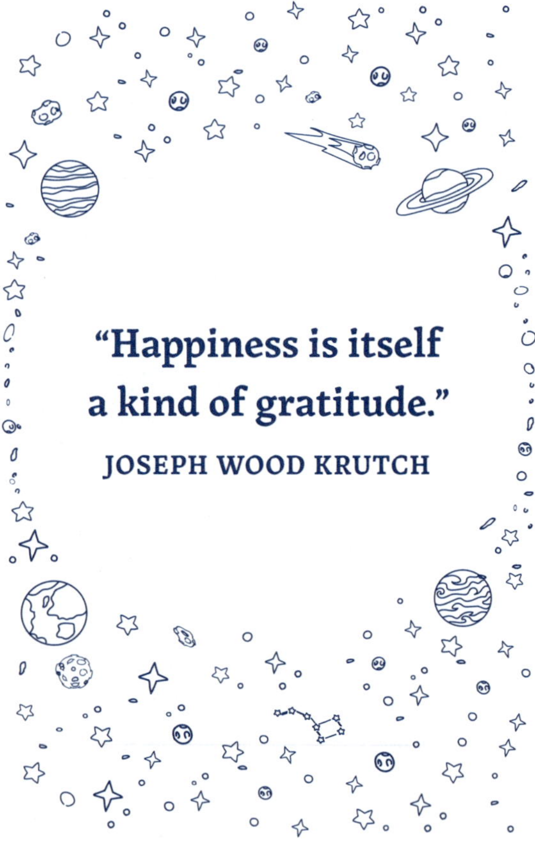

"Happiness is itself a kind of gratitude."

JOSEPH WOOD KRUTCH

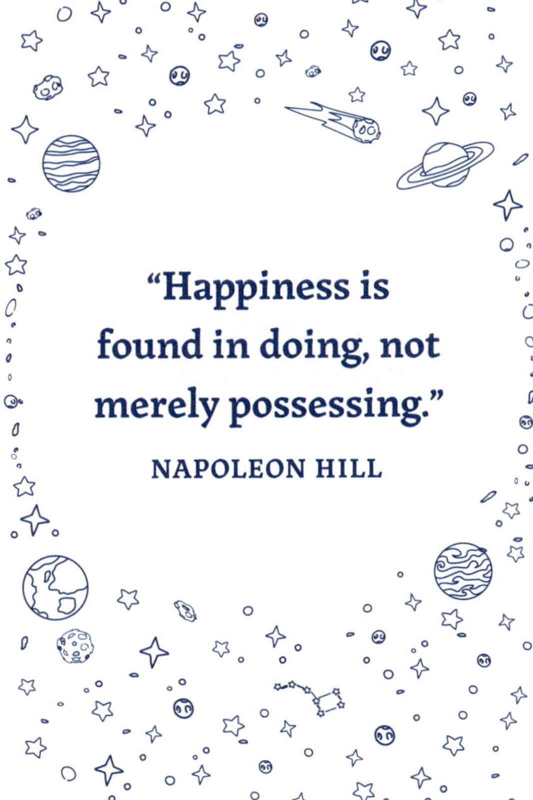

“Happiness is found in doing, not merely possessing.”

NAPOLEON HILL

“DESIRE NOTHING,
GIVE UP ALL DESIRES
AND BE HAPPY.”

SWAMI SIVANANDA

"Happiness is a butterfly, which when pursued, is always just beyond your grasp, but which, if you will sit down quietly, may alight upon you."

NATHANIEL HAWTHORNE

“In times of joy, all of us wished we possessed a tail we could wag.”

W. H. AUDEN

“THE HAPPIEST PEOPLE SEEM TO BE THOSE WHO HAVE NO PARTICULAR CAUSE FOR BEING HAPPY EXCEPT THAT THEY ARE SO.”

WILLIAM INGE

"Peace comes from within.
Do not seek it without."

BUDDHA

"You must try to generate happiness within yourself. If you aren't happy in one place, chances are you won't be happy anyplace."

ERNIE BANKS

"HAPPINESS IS LIKE A CLOUD, IF YOU STARE AT IT LONG ENOUGH, IT EVAPORATES."

SARAH MCLACHLAN

"HAPPY HE WHO LEARNS TO BEAR WHAT HE CANNOT CHANGE."

FRIEDRICH SCHILLER

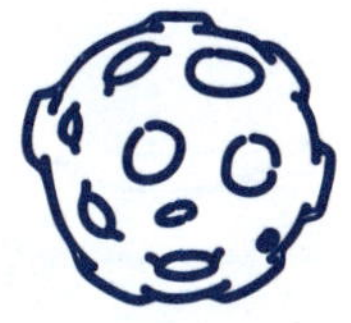

"TO FORGET
ONESELF IS
TO BE HAPPY."
ROBERT LOUIS
STEVENSON

“Happiness depends upon ourselves.”

ARISTOTLE

"HAPPINESS IS WHEN WHAT YOU THINK, WHAT YOU SAY, AND WHAT YOU DO ARE IN HARMONY."

MAHATMA GANDHI

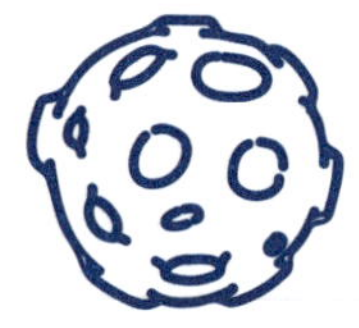

“THE MOMENTS OF HAPPINESS WE ENJOY TAKE US BY SURPRISE. IT IS NOT THAT WE SEIZE THEM, BUT THAT THEY SEIZE US.”

ASHLEY MONTAGU

“EVEN IF
HAPPINESS FORGETS
YOU A LITTLE BIT,
NEVER COMPLETELY
FORGET ABOUT IT.”
JAQUES
PREVERT

"ONE OF THE SECRETS OF A HAPPY LIFE IS CONTINUOUS SMALL TREATS."

IRIS MURDOCH

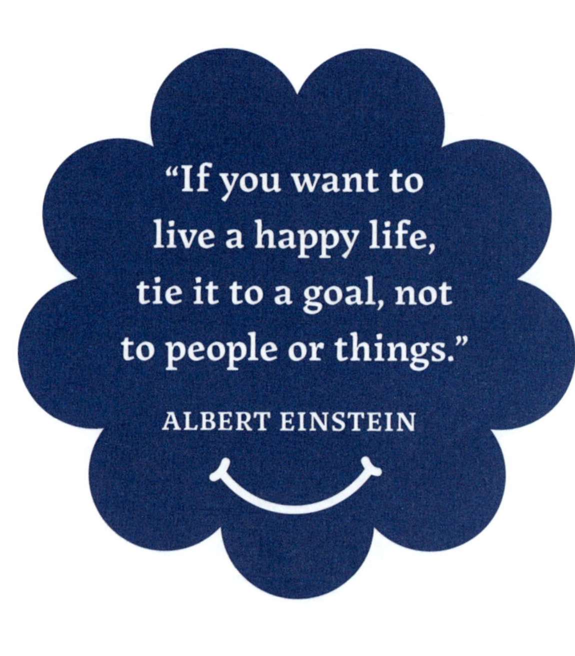
"If you want to
live a happy life,
tie it to a goal, not
to people or things."
ALBERT EINSTEIN

“HAPPINESS CONSISTS NOT IN HAVING MUCH, BUT IN BEING CONTENT WITH LITTLE.”

MARGUERITE,
COUNTESS OF BLESSINGTON

"Carry on, no matter what happens. Hide your sorrows under a smile and carry on."

ANONYMOUS

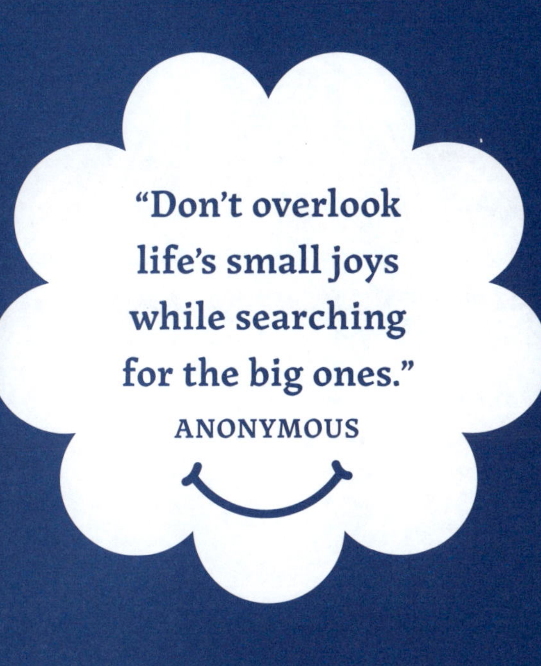
“Don’t overlook
life’s small joys
while searching
for the big ones.”
ANONYMOUS

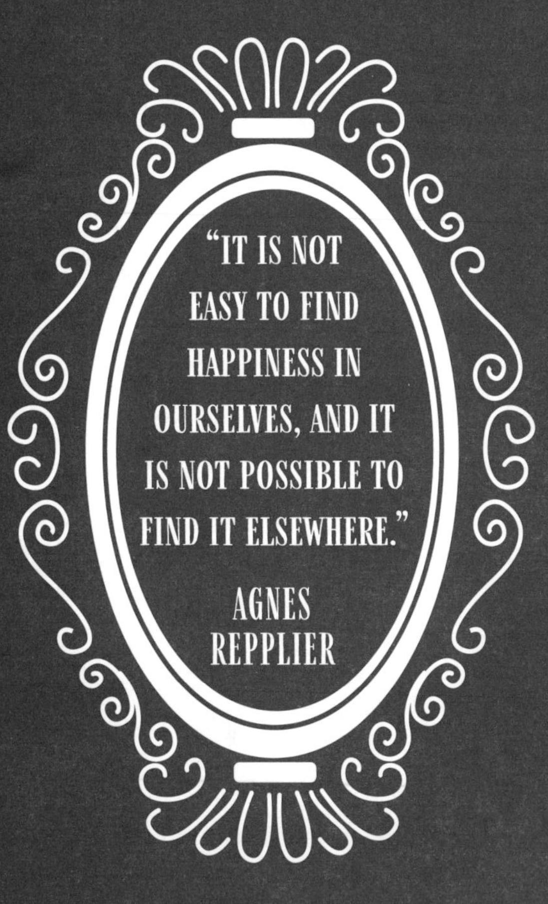
"IT IS NOT
EASY TO FIND
HAPPINESS IN
OURSELVES, AND IT
IS NOT POSSIBLE TO
FIND IT ELSEWHERE."
AGNES
REPPLIER

"WORRY NEVER ROBS TOMORROW OF ITS SORROW; IT ONLY SAPS TODAY OF ITS STRENGTH."

A.J. CRONIN

"FOR EVERY MINUTE YOU ARE ANGRY, YOU LOSE SIXTY SECONDS OF HAPPINESS."

Ralph Waldo Emerson

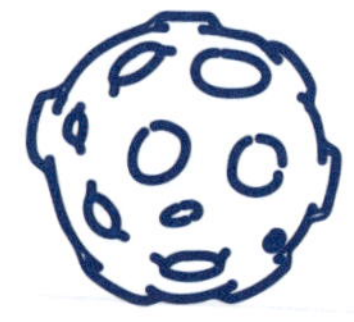

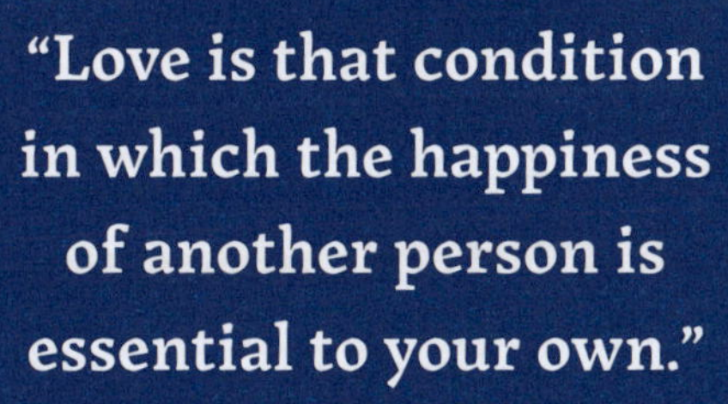
"Love is that condition
in which the happiness
of another person is
essential to your own."
ROBERT A. HEINLEIN

“Folks are usually about as happy as they make their minds up to be.”

ABRAHAM LINCOLN

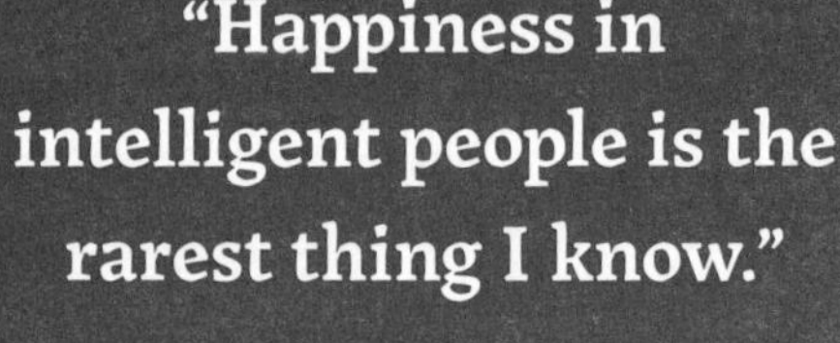

"Happiness in intelligent people is the rarest thing I know."

ERNEST HEMINGWAY

"You will never be happy if you continue to search for what happiness consists of. You will never live if you are looking for the meaning of life."

ALBERT CAMUS

"EVERY MAN HAS HIS SECRET SORROWS WHICH THE WORLD KNOWS NOT; AND OFTEN TIMES WE CALL A MAN COLD WHEN HE IS ONLY SAD."

HENRY WADSWORTH LONGFELLOW

"COUNT YOUR AGE BY FRIENDS, NOT YEARS. COUNT YOUR LIFE BY SMILES, NOT TEARS."

JOHN LENNON

"ATTITUDE IS A CHOICE.
HAPPINESS IS A CHOICE.
OPTIMISM IS A CHOICE.
KINDNESS IS A CHOICE.
GIVING IS A CHOICE.
RESPECT IS A CHOICE.
WHATEVER CHOICE YOU MAKE
MAKES YOU. CHOOSE WISELY."

ROY T. BENNETT

"THE MOST IMPORTANT THING IS TO ENJOY YOUR LIFE—TO BE HAPPY—IT'S ALL THAT MATTERS."

AUDREY HEPBURN

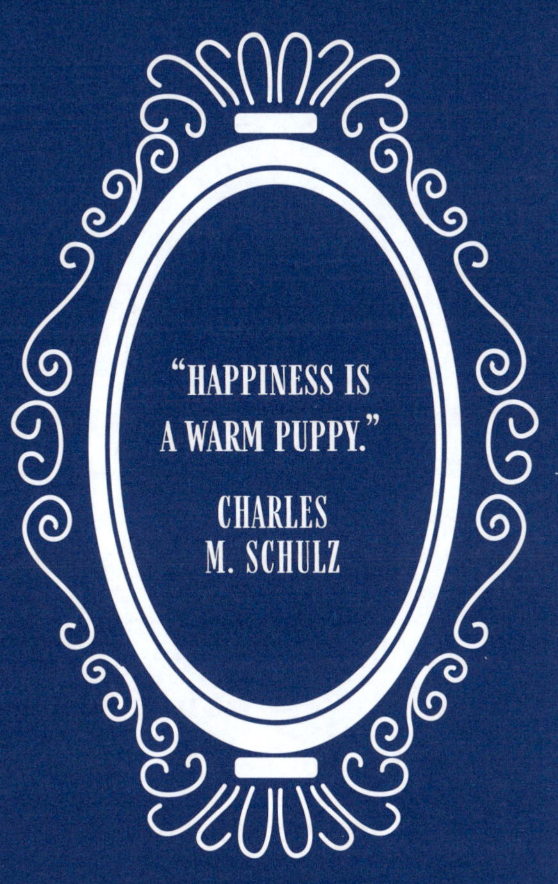
“HAPPINESS IS
A WARM PUPPY.”
CHARLES
M. SCHULZ

"IT ISN'T WHAT YOU HAVE OR WHO YOU ARE OR WHERE YOU ARE OR WHAT YOU ARE DOING THAT MAKES YOU HAPPY OR UNHAPPY. IT IS WHAT YOU THINK ABOUT IT."

DALE CARNEGIE

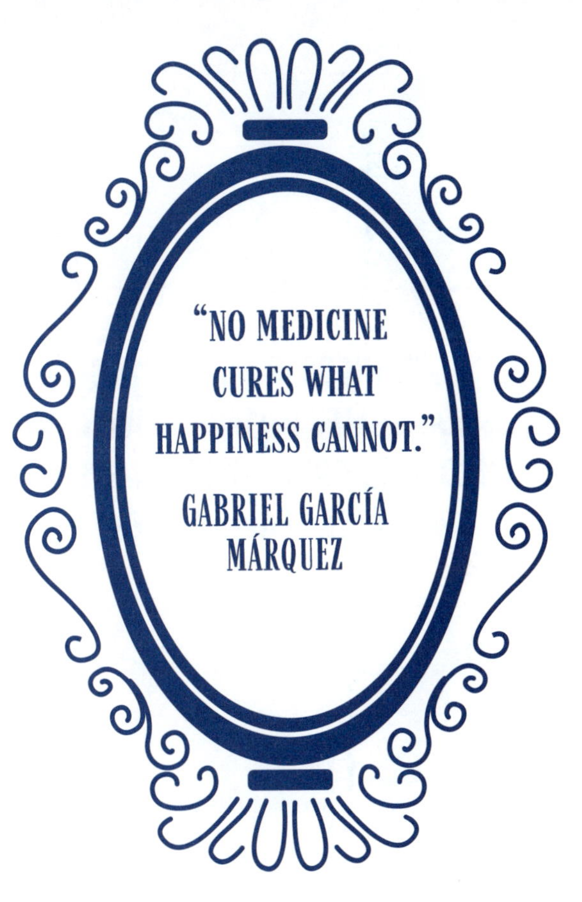
"NO MEDICINE
CURES WHAT
HAPPINESS CANNOT."
GABRIEL GARCÍA
MÁRQUEZ

"HAPPINESS IS SOMETHING THAT COMES INTO OUR LIVES THROUGH DOORS WE DON'T EVEN REMEMBER LEAVING OPEN."

ROSE LANE

t's been my experience that
ou can nearly always enjoy
things if you make up your
mind firmly that you will."

LUCY MAUD
MONTGOMERY

"I felt my lungs inflate with
the onrush of scenery—air,
mountains, trees, people. I thought,
'This is what it is to be happy.'"

SYLVIA PLATH

"Hope smiles from the threshold of the year to come, whispering 'it will be happier' . . ."

ALFRED, LORD TENNYSON

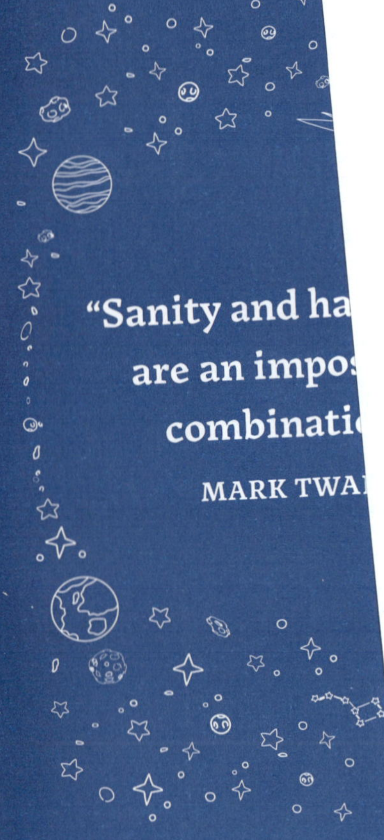

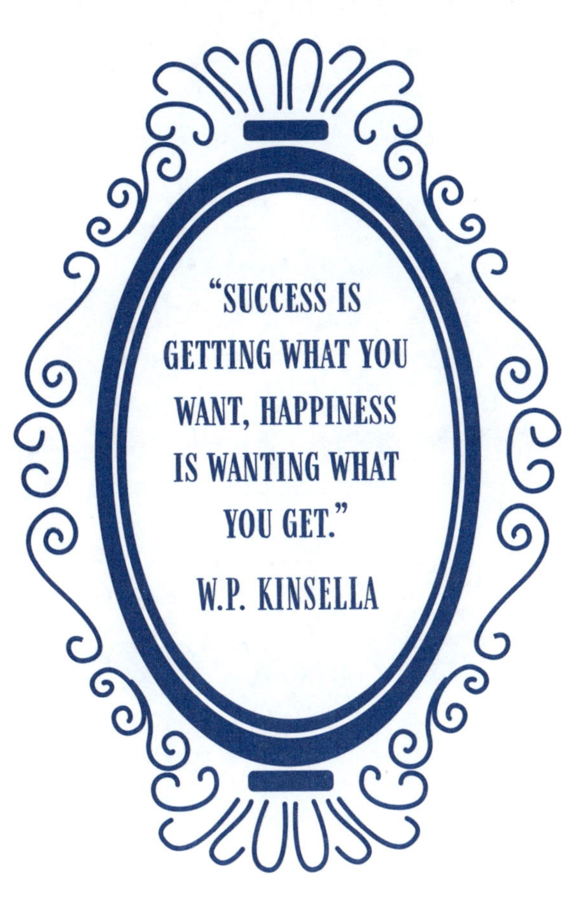
"SUCCESS IS
GETTING WHAT YOU
WANT, HAPPINESS
IS WANTING WHAT
YOU GET."
W.P. KINSELLA

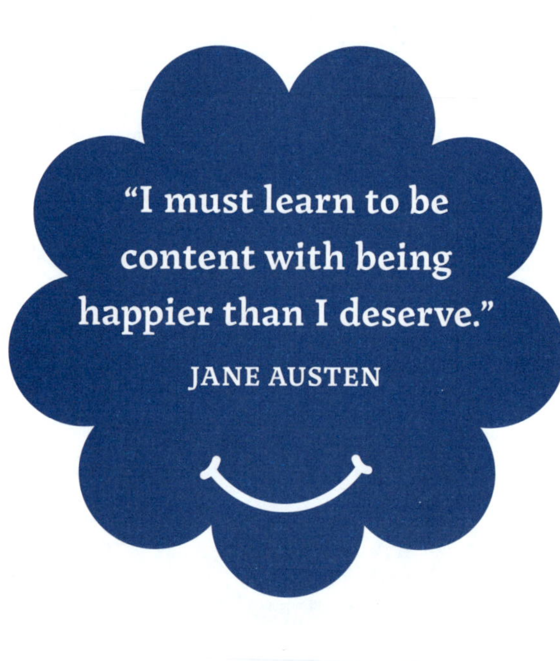
"I must learn to be content with being happier than I deserve."
JANE AUSTEN

“MAN ONLY LIKES TO COUNT HIS TROUBLES; HE DOESN’T CALCULATE HIS HAPPINESS.”

FYODOR DOSTOEVSKY

"Happiness
is a state of mind.
It's just according
to the way you
look at things."

WALT DISNEY

"I felt my lungs inflate with
the onrush of scenery—air,
mountains, trees, people. I thought,
'This is what it is to be happy.'"

SYLVIA PLATH

"Hope smiles from the threshold of the year to come, whispering 'it will be happier' . . ."

ALFRED, LORD TENNYSON

"It's been my experience that you can nearly always enjoy things if you make up your mind firmly that you will."

LUCY MAUD MONTGOMERY

“Sanity and happiness are an impossible combination.”

MARK TWAIN

"MAN ONLY LIKES TO COUNT HIS TROUBLES; HE DOESN'T CALCULATE HIS HAPPINESS."

FYODOR DOSTOEVSKY

"Happiness is a state of mind. It's just according to the way you look at things."

WALT DISNEY

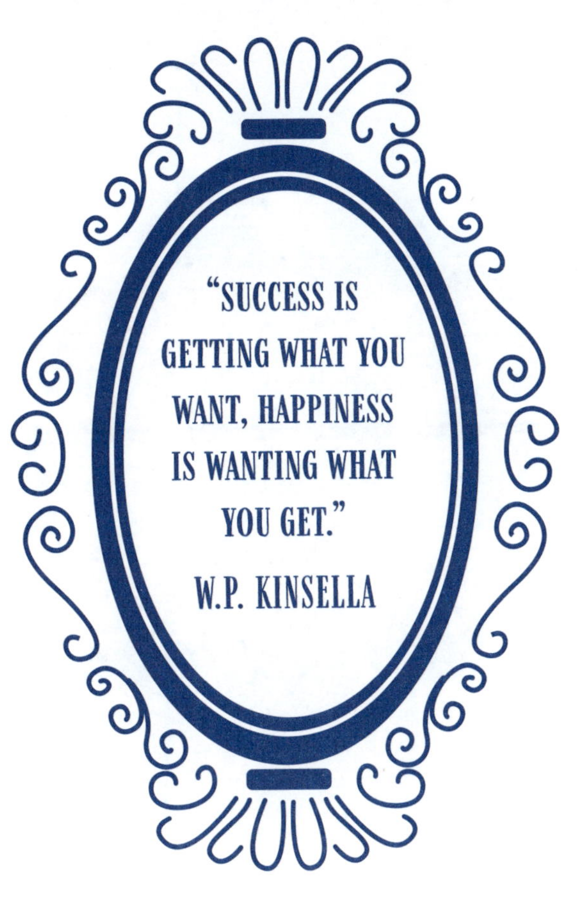
"SUCCESS IS
GETTING WHAT YOU
WANT, HAPPINESS
IS WANTING WHAT
YOU GET."
W.P. KINSELLA

"I must learn to be
content with being
happier than I deserve."
JANE AUSTEN

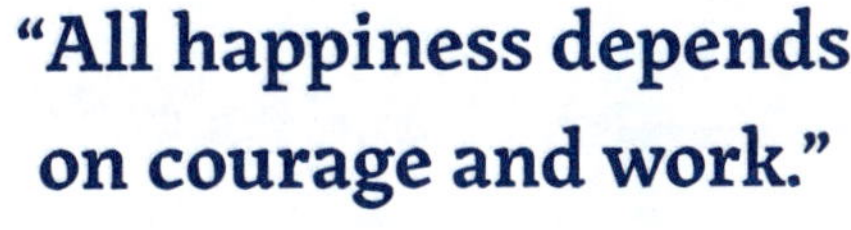

"All happiness depends on courage and work."

HONORÉ DE BALZAC

"Happiness is
like a kiss.
You must share it
to enjoy it."

BERNARD MELTZER

"Happiness is letting go
of what you think your life
is supposed to look like
and celebrating it for
everything that it is."

MANDY HALE

"IT WAS ONLY A SUNNY SMILE,
AND LITTLE IT COST IN THE GIVING,
BUT LIKE MORNING LIGHT IT
SCATTERED THE NIGHT AND
MADE THE DAY WORTH LIVING."

F. SCOTT FITZGERALD

"I don't know what's worse:
to not know what you are and
be happy, or to become what you've
always wanted to be, and feel alone."

DANIEL KEYES

"And hand in hand,
on the edge of the sand,
They danced by the
light of the moon."
EDWARD LEAR

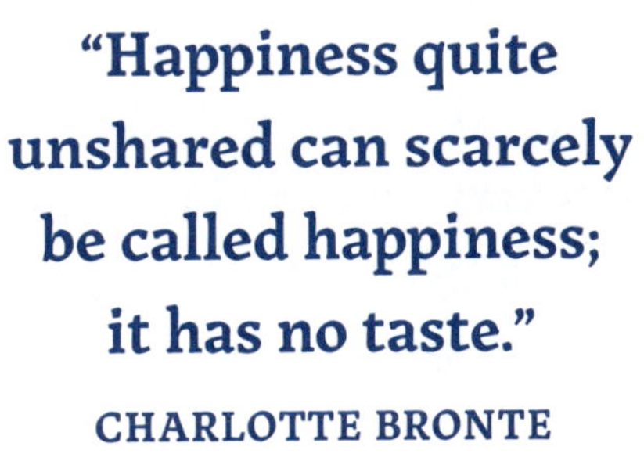

“Happiness quite unshared can scarcely be called happiness; it has no taste.”

CHARLOTTE BRONTE

“THE KEY TO BEING HAPPY IS KNOWING YOU HAVE THE POWER TO CHOOSE WHAT TO ACCEPT AND WHAT TO LET GO.”

DODINSKY

"Actual happiness always looks pretty squalid in comparison with the overcompensations for misery. And, of course, stability isn't nearly so spectacular as instability. And being contented has none of the glamour of a good fight against misfortune, none of the picturesqueness of a struggle with temptation, or a fatal overthrow bypassion or doubt. Happiness is never grand."

ALDOUS HUXLEY

"I felt once more how simple and frugal a thing is happiness: a glass of wine, a roast chestnut, a wretched little brazier, the sound of the sea. Nothing else."

NIKOS KAZANTZAKIS

"Happiness is the experience
of loving life. Being happy is being in
love with that momentary experience.
And love is looking at someone
or even something and seeing
the absolute best in him/her or it.
Love is happiness with what you see.
So love and happiness really are the
same thing...just expressed differently."

ROBERT MCPHILLIPS

"Generally speaking, the most miserable people I know are those who are obsessed with themselves; the happiest people I know are those who lose themselves in the service of others . . . By and large, I have come to see that if we complain about life, it is because we are thinking only of ourselves."

GORDON B. HINCKLEY

"HAPPINESS IS THE MEANING AND THE PURPOSE OF LIFE, THE WHOLE AIM AND END OF HUMAN EXISTENCE."

ARISTOTLE

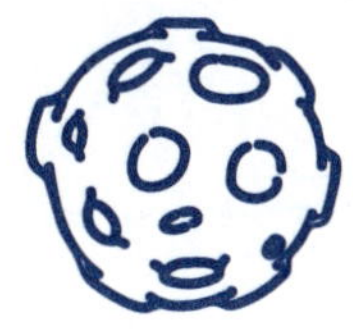

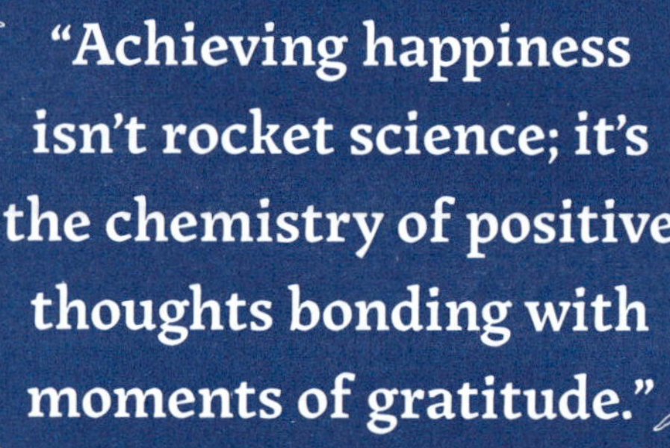
"Achieving happiness
isn't rocket science; it's
the chemistry of positive
thoughts bonding with
moments of gratitude."

SHAWN ACHOR

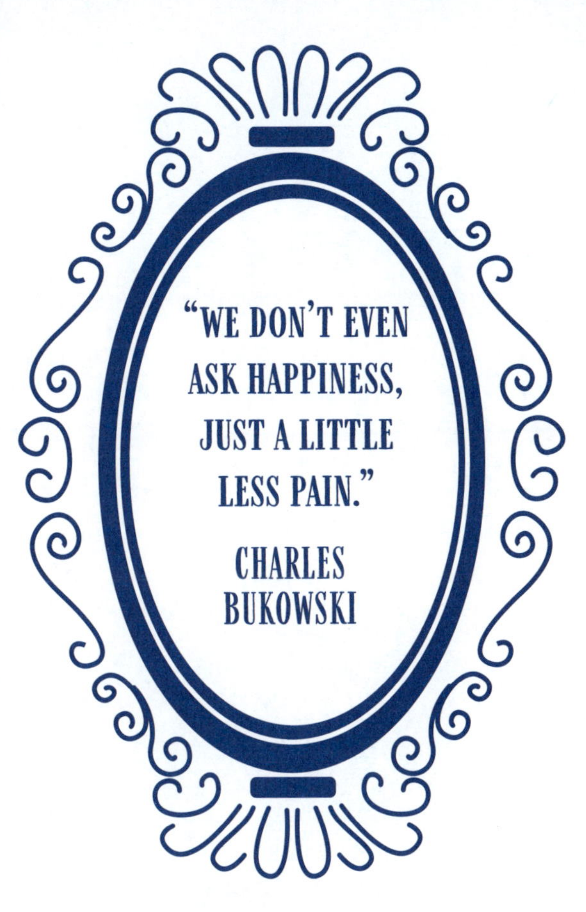
"WE DON'T EVEN
ASK HAPPINESS,
JUST A LITTLE
LESS PAIN."
CHARLES
BUKOWSKI

"THERE ARE TWO WAYS TO GET ENOUGH. ONE IS TO CONTINUE TO ACCUMULATE MORE AND MORE. THE OTHER IS TO DESIRE LESS."

G.K. CHESTERTON

"Sadness gives depth. Happiness gives height. Sadness gives roots. Happiness gives branches. Happiness is like a tree going into the sky, and sadness is like the roots going down into the womb of the earth. Both are needed, and the higher a tree goes, the deeper it goes, simultaneously. The bigger the tree, the bigger will be its roots. In fact, it is always in proportion. That's its balance."

OSHO

"THOSE WHO ARE NOT LOOKING FOR HAPPINESS ARE THE MOST LIKELY TO FIND IT, BECAUSE THOSE WHO ARE SEARCHING FORGET THAT THE SUREST WAY TO BE HAPPY IS TO SEEK HAPPINESS FOR OTHERS."

MARTIN LUTHER KING JR.

"HAPPINESS IS AN ACCIDENT OF NATURE, A BEAUTIFUL AND FLAWLESS ABERRATION."

PAT CONROY

"The myriad things are complete in us. There is no greater joy than to reflect on ourselves and become sincere."

MENCIUS

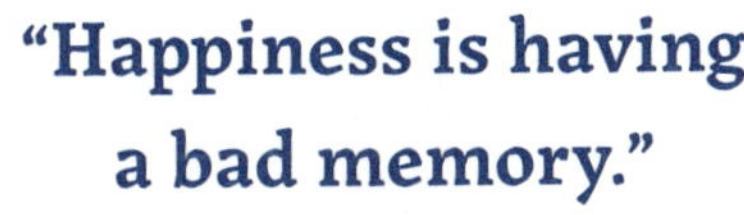

"Happiness is having a bad memory."

INGRID BERGMAN

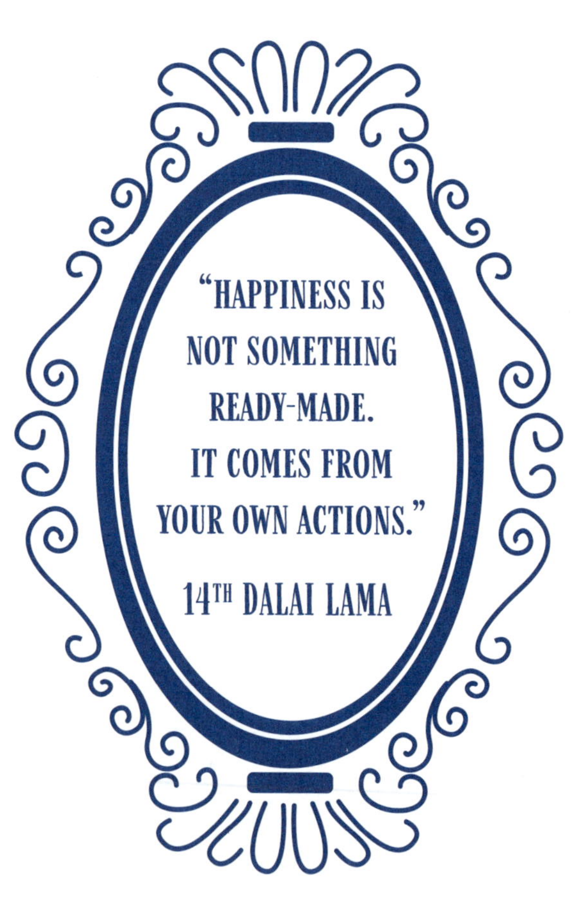
"HAPPINESS IS
NOT SOMETHING
READY-MADE.
IT COMES FROM
YOUR OWN ACTIONS."
14TH DALAI LAMA

"The secret to happiness
is not in doing what one likes to do,
but in liking what one has to do."

JAMES M. BARRIE

"THE GREATEST HAPPINESS YOU CAN HAVE IS KNOWING THAT YOU DO NOT NECESSARILY REQUIRE HAPPINESS."

WILLIAM SAROYAN

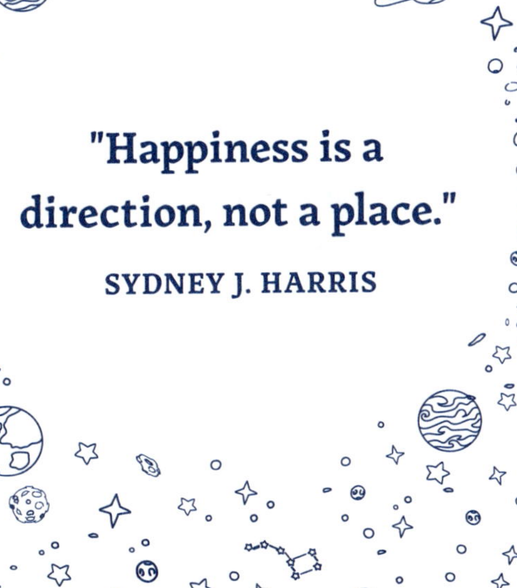
"Happiness is a
direction, not a place."
SYDNEY J. HARRIS

"THE ONLY THING THAT WILL MAKE YOU HAPPY IS BEING HAPPY WITH WHO YOU ARE, AND NOT WHO PEOPLE THINK YOU ARE."

GOLDIE HAWN

"Happiness is not in the mere possession of money; it lies in the joy of achievement, in the thrill of creative effort."

FRANKLIN D. ROOSEVELT

"THE ONLY WAY TO FIND TRUE HAPPINESS IS TO RISK BEING COMPLETELY CUT OPEN."

CHUCK PALAHNIUK

“Happiness is not the absence of problems; it’s the ability to deal with them.”

STEVE MARABOLI

"THE TRUE SECRET OF HAPPINESS LIES IN TAKING A GENUINE INTEREST IN ALL THE DETAILS OF DAILY LIFE."

WILLIAM MORRIS